TRADITIONS AND CELEBRATIONS

ROSH HASHANAH

by Gloria Koster

PEBBLE
a capstone imprint

Published by Pebble, an imprint of Capstone
1710 Roe Crest Drive, North Mankato, Minnesota 56003
capstonepub.com

Library of Congress Cataloging-in-Publication Data is available
on the Library of Congress website.
ISBN: 9780756575892 (hardcover)
ISBN: 9780756575847 (paperback)
ISBN: 9780756575854 (ebook PDF)

Summary: Rosh Hashanah, the Jewish New Year, is the first of the Jewish
Holy High Days and one of Judaism's holiest days. Often called the birthday
of the world, it is celebrated on the first day of Tishrei, the seventh month of
the Hebrew calendar. People celebrate this happy holiday with family and
friends by praying, lighting candles, and eating special meals and sweet
treats. Learn more about the history behind this important day and how
it's observed today.

Editorial Credits
Editor: Alison Deering; Designer: Jaime Willems; Media Researcher:
Rebekah Hubstenberger; Production Specialist: Whitney Schaefer

Image Credits
Getty Images: emyerson, 11, GIL COHEN-MAGEN/AFP, 14, Hill Street
Studios, 29, iStock/Dusan Stankovic, 13, Mark Boster/Los Angeles Times,
18, Nathan Bilow, 17, Rafael Ben-Ari, 25, Robert Nicholas, 7, Sima_ha,
5; Shutterstock: Allexxandar, 9, Iryna Tolmachova, 4, Joanna Dorota, 28,
Monkey Business Images, 1, 21, 27, Ozgur Senergin, 23, Pixel-Shot, 20,
Sokor Space, cover, Trofimchuk Vladimir, 10, Viktoria Hodos, 24

Design Elements
Shutterstock: Rafal Kulik

Printed and bound in China. PO5379

TABLE OF CONTENTS

Words in **bold** are in the glossary.

WHAT IS ROSH HASHANAH?

Summer is over. The days are cooler now. In some places, the leaves are changing colors. Kids are back in school. But on Rosh Hashanah, some schools are closed. This is the Jewish New Year.

Some schools are closed on Rosh Hashanah.

**Apples and honey are common
Rosh Hashanah foods.**

Rosh Hashanah is a happy holiday. It is like a birthday celebration. It celebrates the creation of the world.

Some Jewish people observe this holiday for two days. Others celebrate for just one day. Families get together with friends and loved ones. They enjoy special meals and sweet treats. They wish for a sweet new year.

Rosh Hashanah has a serious side too. People visit their **synagogue** to pray. They think about mistakes they have made. They ask for God's forgiveness. They promise to do better in the coming year.

Jewish people believe that on Rosh Hashanah, God opens a special book. This is called the Book of Life. While the book is open, God hears each person's prayers. Then he decides each person's **fate**.

After 10 days, the book is closed. God's decisions are final. The day the book is closed is called **Yom Kippur**. Rosh Hashanah and Yom Kippur are both High Holy Days.

WHEN IS ROSH HASHANAH?

Seven is an important number in Judaism. Jewish people believe the world was created in seven days. That is why Rosh Hashanah begins on the first day of the seventh month of the Jewish calendar. It is a lunar-solar calendar. It has twelve months. It follows phases of the moon and sun.

Jewish holidays take place in certain seasons. Rosh Hashanah takes place in the fall. The dates change from year to year. Some years it is in September. Other years it is in October.

The phases of the moon

Most people think of each day beginning at sunrise. But Jewish days begin when the sun sets. Holidays start the evening before the first day.

The sun sets over a synagogue.

Every Jewish holiday begins with a blessing for the wine and the bread. On Rosh Hashanah eve, families gather. They light candles and say a prayer. They bless wine and **challah** bread. After blessings, it's time for a delicious holiday dinner.

GETTING READY

Holiday preparations begin the month before Rosh Hashanah. The new year is coming. It is a great time for a fresh start. People apologize to others. They imagine the best they can be.

Children think of ways they can improve. They draw pictures to show their good deeds. People send out greeting cards. They take new family pictures. On the street, they greet each other by saying, "Shana Tova!" That means "have a good year."

A ram's horn is made into a shofar.

In synagogue, someone blows the **shofar**. This is a ram's horn. It makes a loud sound. It's a wake-up call. It reminds people that Rosh Hashanah is almost here.

In different parts of the world, there are different traditions. Some go back to ancient times. Syrian men would always get a haircut before Rosh Hashanah. This represented getting rid of sins from the year before.

Buying a new knife is an old European tradition. A knife is a symbol for a year of plenty.

A DAY TO PRAY

Families go to synagogue on Rosh Hashanah morning. They hear three sets of prayers. After each set, people hear the shofar. It reminds them to look inside themselves.

The **rabbi** is the religious leader. He or she reads from the **Torah**. On Rosh Hashanah, the rabbi reads about Abraham, the father of the Jewish religion. The story is about having faith in God.

A rabbi reads from the Torah.

Getting rid of sin is an important part of Rosh Hashanah.

There is also an afternoon ceremony. It takes place at a body of flowing water. People come to throw away their sins. They promise to do better in the new year. Some turn their pockets inside-out. Bits of lint represent their **regrets**.

Some people throw breadcrumbs or pieces of bread into the water. But human food can harm wildlife. It's better to toss pebbles or twigs. Leaves or bird seed are okay too.

HOLIDAY FOODS

On Rosh Hashanah, people eat apples dipped in honey. Apples have no leaves for protection. Still, they survive. This is just like the Jewish people. The honey makes the apples taste even sweeter.

During Rosh Hashanah,
challah is round.

Jewish people eat challah throughout
the year. On Rosh Hashanah, the
challah must have a special shape.
It is round like the circle of life.
Sometimes it also has raisins
for extra sweetness.

Not all Jewish families enjoy the same holiday foods. That's because Jewish people have **ancestors** from different places. Ashkenazi Jews have ancestors from Northern and Central Europe. Sephardic Jews have ancestors from Spain and Portugal.

During Rosh Hashanah, Sephardic Jews hold a **Seder**. The foods served at this special meal are symbols. Pomegranates are filled with seeds. Lots of seeds mean lots of good luck. Seeds are also a symbol of new life. Other symbolic foods are pumpkins, green beans, and dates.

a pomegranate

apple cake with honey

Rosh Hashanah dinner often includes chicken or **brisket**. Tzimmes is a yummy side dish. It's a sweet carrot stew. Apple cake and honey cake are popular desserts.

Some people place a fish head on the dinner table. People hope to get ahead in life. The head also stands for Rosh Hashanah. This holiday heads off a brand-new year.

ROSH HASHANAH PROJECTS

Rosh Hashanah is a time for family activities. Before the holiday, it's fun to visit an apple orchard. Homemade applesauce or apple cake make the house smell wonderful. So does a freshly baked challah!

There are many Rosh Hashanah craft projects. It's fun to decorate holiday cards with apple prints. It's also fun to make placemats or napkin rings for the holiday table.

Jewish people believe in making the world a better place. Rosh Hashanah is not just about improving ourselves. It's about helping others too. The new year is an excellent time donate food or clothing. It is also a good time to volunteer in the community.

GLOSSARY

ancestor (AN-sess-tur)—a family member who lived a long time ago

challah (HAH-luh)—an egg-rich yeast-leavened bread that is usually braided or twisted before baking and is traditionally eaten by Jewish people on holidays

fate (FEYT)—events in a person's life that are beyond control or are determined by a supernatural power

rabbi (RAB-ahy)—a professionally trained leader of a Jewish congregation

regret (ri-GRET)—a feeling of sorrow or remorse

Seder (SEY-der)—a Jewish ceremonial dinner

shofar (SHOH-fer)—a horn blown as a trumpet during Jewish religious occasions, especially during Rosh Hashanah and at the end of Yom Kippur

synagogue (SIN-a-gog)—a building where Jewish people come together to pray

Torah (TOH-ruh)—a scroll containing the first five books of the Old Testament used in a synagogue for religious services

Yom Kippur (YAWM ki-POOR)—a Jewish holiday observed in September or October with fasting and prayer as ways of making up for sins

READ MORE

Mara, Wil. *Holidays Around the World*. North Mankato, MN: Capstone, 2021.

Richardson, Betsy. *Marking the Religious New Year*. Broomall, PA: Mason Crest, 2018.

Rubinstein, Elana. *Once Upon an Apple Cake: A Rosh Hashanah Story*. Millburn, NJ: Apples & Honey Press, 2019.

INTERNET SITES

My Jewish Learning: Rosh Hashanah 101
myjewishlearning.com/article/rosh-hashanah-101

PJ Library: Simanim: The Symbolic Foods of Rosh Hashanah
pjlibrary.org/beyond-books/pjblog/september-2014/simanim-the-symbolic-foods-of-rosh-hashanah

The Jewish Children's Learning Network: Rosh Hashanah Traditions
akhlah.com/jewish-holidays/roshhashanah/rosh-hashanah-traditions

INDEX

ABOUT THE AUTHOR

photo by Eric Koster

A public and a school librarian, Gloria belongs to the Children's Book Committee of Bank Street College of Education. She enjoys both city and country life, dividing her time between Manhattan and the small town of Pound Ridge, New York. Gloria has three adult children and a bunch of energetic grandkids.